Land Buying Tips

How to Buy Rural

Written & Compiled by Pat Porter

Table of Contents

List of Contributors

Below is a list of the land pros who've contributed to this book. Their professional and personal information is at the end of each of their chapters.

To some degree, each of the land brokers listed here are competitors. That said, we all work well with one another, respect each other's knowledge and businesses and support each other in the land industry. We frequently share information and work together in land transactions. Please feel free to contact any of them to inquire of their services.

Rick Taylor - Broker/Owner of Mossy Oak Properties Forest Investments, Inc. in McComb, Mississippi.

Jim Rolfe - Licensed professional real estate agent in multiple states for Brown Realty Company in Rayville, Louisiana.

Scott Lindsey - Forester and Broker/Owner of United Country Gibson Realty and Land in McComb, Mississippi.

Brandon White - Forester and Associate Broker with RecLand Realty, LLC in Jasper, Texas.

Lannie B. Philley - Land Manager for Delta Land & Farm Management, Co. LLC in Mer Rouge, Louisiana.

Rockland (Rocky) Burks – Forester and Owner/Broker of Rockland R. Burks, Inc. in Monroe, Louisiana.

Paul Hurd – Licensed attorney and Owner/Title Agent of Home Title Guaranty in Monroe, Louisiana.

Ryan Folk – Founder/Owner of the LANDFLIP network in Madison, Georgia.

Pat Porter – Owner/Broker of RecLand Realty, LLC in Monroe, Louisiana

Introduction

If you get good information, you can make a good decision. This book's goal is to give you some good information about many different aspects of buying rural land.

I called eight top land professionals and asked them to each write a chapter about a specific subject that would help people in their land-buying process. I, too, added a chapter. The resulting book is a no-fluff resource that addresses many of the questions land buyers have.

There is no theory here. This information comes from combined decades of experience and combined hundreds of millions of dollars of land transactions from the contributors. The information offered here has been fleshed out in the real world of timberland, farm land, recreational properties, development tracts and closing tables where people have bought and sold thousands of acres of rural real estate.

Each writer puts forth his information from his own unique prospective and in his own style. You'll read Jim Rolfe's guide to buying hunting land in the Midwest written in a no-nonsense manner, as well as Paul Hurd's calculated, carefully chosen phrasing, walking you through a review of your need for title insurance…and every style and personality in between.

The book is written in such a way that you can skip around from chapter to chapter and get good information about the specific subjects you have interest in. I'd recommend, however, that you read it straight through. Sure, you may find yourself reading about a type of land you are not currently pursuing purchasing. But you will gain a deeper overall understanding of how to approach rural real estate – like these guys do – and this will likely cause you to look at your next purchase in a different way. You'll pick up on common threads that each writer mentions that seem to apply across many potential land buys.

Well, let's get on with it. Take a look at the good information in the first chapter of "Land Buying Tips from the Pros."

Chapter 1 - Timberland Investment – The Crucial Number to Know - By Rick Taylor

Not long ago, a writer working on an article discussing timberland as an investment asked me a good question. He wanted to know what I thought were the two most important factors in evaluating the investment potential of a particular timberland tract. It's very hard to narrow it down to just two, but I told him the most important factors were the proximity to area mills and site index.

The proximity to area mills is a no-brainer. When forest products are purchased from a landowner (timberland investor), certain costs of production must be considered. There are many factors that affect production cost, but the distance to the mills is likely the most important. The further the owner's property is from the mill, the more it will cost to get his product from the stump to the mill.

The extra distance means extra expense to the logger – and that means less money available to be paid to the timber owner. This amount, the money paid to the timber owner, is referred to as "stumpage". Because there is a finite amount a company can pay for the raw material and remain profitable, any additional expense incurred by the logger will have to come from the amount that can be paid to the timber owner.

Timberland investors can contact their state Forestry Extension Service office to get locations of area mills. You can also talk with foresters in your area to get information about the timber market where you own or may want to buy timberland. They not only know where all the mills are, but they will also know which ones are the best for the type of product you will be selling.

Proximity to area mills is pretty easy to understand. Now I want to spend some time discussing the other major factor – the site index. But before we look at what site index is and how it impacts the investment potential of timberland, let me point out something you may not have considered: is your real estate agent knowledgeable of and qualified to represent you in a timberland transaction?

Why should this be your first consideration? Well, Article 11 of the National Association of Realtors' Code of Ethics and Standards of Practice states in part: "Realtors shall not undertake to provide specialized professional services concerning a type of property or service that is outside their field of competence unless they engage the assistance of one who is competent on such types of property or service, or unless the facts are fully disclosed to the client."

Any Realtor attempting to sell a timberland tract, whether representing the buyer or the seller, who does not know what site index is, its relevance, and how it relates to the particular tracts you may be interested in seeing is violating the Realtor Code of Ethics. If you are being represented by a real estate professional regarding the purchase or sale of a timberland tract, try this litmus test. Just ask them what "site index" is. Ask them why it's relevant and what the site index of the particular property you are looking at is. Their answer will tell the tale!

I may not fully understand the cap rate on a four-story office complex in uptown Manhattan, but I don't sell commercial buildings in New York. I do however, sell and manage timberland in the southeast, so I do understand site index. Get a professional who understands the specifics about the type of property you want so you can get good information to make informed buying decisions.

No prudent land professional should attempt to sell a timberland property without knowing its site index. I think you can tell this is something that I feel very strongly about. Here's a link to the ethics code I mentioned.
http://www.realtor.org/sites/default/files/policies/2016/2016-NAR-Code-of-Ethics.pdf.

So what exactly is site index? Site index is a measurement of the ability of a particular soil to grow a particular species of tree to a certain height over a certain number of years. Stated differently, it is the average height, in feet, that dominant and codominant trees of a given species attain in a specified number of years.

Typically, 50 years is the standard time that is used in the site index measurement. However, timber companies growing timber on short rotations (the period from planting to final harvest) will often use a 25-year index. So let's be sure we're clear. A site index of 90 means that the soil occupying that site will grow a particular species of tree 90 feet tall in 50 years.

As I continue to explain the importance of site index, it is important that a buyer understands that a site index that is considered premium in one area of the country may be just average in another area. For example, in the area where I live and work, a site index of 100 or greater is common and considered excellent. A site index of 80 may be considered excellent in other areas. It's all relative to where you want to be and what kind of return you are expecting.

To illustrate my point, I want to look at the return on a pine plantation using different site indices. The Mississippi Forestry Commission Publication #80 compares site indices of 70, 85, and 100. This publication looks at the total income of a pine plantation over a 35-year rotation. Here's a link to the chart: http://www.mfc.ms.gov/sites/default/files/80-07%20How%20Much%20Is%20Your%20Pine%20Plantation%20Worth_0.pdf.

Using the parameters shown in the publication, the property with an average site index of 70 has an average return per acre per year of $44.69. The property with a site index of 85 has an average return per acre per year of $107.82. The property with a site index of 100 has an average return per acre per year of $262.32. Did you notice how the increase is exponential as the site index increases? This should get your attention. Exponential growth in returns is what we all want in our land purchases.

This publication illustrates the income from harvests at years 15, 22, and 35 in the life of the plantation. Imagine the value of the investment if you were to re-invest the income from the thinnings you performed in years 15 and 22. Kind of reminds me of the compounding interest examples I saw (about 20 years too late!).

Now you know what site index is and how it is relevant to your investment. Now, how do you find out the site index of a particular property? Site index tables have been developed that allow you to compare the average height and age of the dominant trees on each soil type to the curve shown on the site index table and determine the 50- or 25-year site index. This would require you to know the age and the total height of the trees you measure as well as the soil type they are growing on. Fortunately, just as soil maps for most locations in the United States have been developed, site index tables have been created as well.

This is another little test for your Realtor or land agent. Do they know where to get this information? There are several sources of soil data. One of the better ones is AgriData, Inc. AgriData has soil maps and updated soil data which can be invaluable in evaluating a prospective farm purchase. However, AgriData does not provide site index information, and that's what we're after here. The best source for obtaining site index data remains the United States Department of Agriculture's NRCS Office.

The NRCS (National Resources Conservation Service) used to be called the U.S. Soil Conservation Service. They have developed a website that provides a myriad of usable information on the soils of any property you're likely to want to look at, including site index, and the most suitable timber species for growing on that site. The website can be a little tricky to navigate, but the information is there, along with the ability to quickly zero in on the exact location you want, draw boundaries around the tracts, calculate acreages, and print out excellent maps and reports.

This NRCS soil site is found at http://websoilsurvey.sc.egov.usda.gov/App/HomePage.htm. Just open the site and click on the big green button to take you to the map of the U.S. to get started.

Keep this little piece of information in mind when looking at site index charts: they were developed using measurements from naturally grown trees. Most plantations today, however, are planted with genetically improved seedlings. This can improve the site index from 5% to 20% depending on the seedling source and the level of genetic improvement. Remember how the tree volume/value grew exponentially? Think of the difference there would be between a site index of 100 and 115. Genetically improved seedlings and proper timber management would most likely make those increases appear conservative. Talk to a certified forester to get more information on improved seedlings.

You have to consider a lot of factors when making a timberland investment. The general location of the property, neighbors, and recreational uses would be among these. The transition of a property to a higher and better use will be the ultimate determinant of value, but site index is crucial when looking strictly at the ability of that property to grow and produce wood fiber and generate income. Your reason for purchase may be primarily for recreational and hunting use, but if two properties are priced similarly and have equal recreational value, yet one has a higher site index, the decision on which one to purchase just got easier – at least for you, since you're aware of the value of knowing the site index!

These days you can't turn on a TV without seeing a commercial recommending that you buy gold. I like to tell my clients that we don't know what gold or timber will be worth 10 years from now, but there is one thing I do know: 10 years from now a pound of gold will still be a pound of gold; but a timber stand could easily have twice the volume of wood fiber it had 10 years earlier.

Know your site index and invest wisely!

About Rick Taylor

Rick Taylor is Broker/Owner of Mossy Oak Properties Forest Investments, Inc. in McComb, Mississippi. Rick is a registered forester and has been practicing forestry since graduating in Forestry from Louisiana Tech University in 1979. He obtained his real estate license in 1988 and has been operating a forestry consulting and real estate business since then. His firm deals only in timber, recreational, and farm land, and has three times been awarded Mossy Oak Properties' "Office of the Year." Rick is an Accredited Land Consultant and wrote the REALTORS Land Institute's course "Timberland: Identifying and Evaluating Timberland Investments." He was awarded Mississippi's "Land Realtor of the Year" in 2010 and RLI's "Instructor of the Year" in 2011. He and his wife Tammy live in McComb, MS, and can be reached at 601-341-1131 or rtaylor@mossyoakproperties.com. His website is www.mopforestinvestments.com.

Chapter 2 - Things to Know About Buying Land in the Midwest...If You're Not from the Midwest - By Jim Rolfe

I have spent all of my life hunting and fishing in the Deep South here in northeast Louisiana. It is truly "The Sportsman's Paradise." In the 1980s, we started to take some steps to try to develop some trophy-size whitetail bucks in our herd. We simply started shooting more does and passing on the bucks. Keep in mind, this management practice was not the strategy we grew up with as kids, and a lot of the older folks certainly didn't do it that way…and a few still don't! But it was our start into managing deer for better quality.

Fast forward to 2016. We have more acres of CRP and WRP than ever before in our state. These are U.S. Department of Agriculture programs that convert poorer farm ground back to wildlife habitat and permanent wetlands. This creates more permanent cover for deer and other wildlife. We also have more farmland acres dedicated to the grain crops for the deer's diet. These big changes in the habitat, along with passing on the younger bucks and harvesting more does, resulted in our seeing improvement in the older age classes and antler size of whitetail bucks in our region. There are giants killed every year all over our state now. I've even killed a couple of 150" class bucks here. The giants are still hard to come by, though!

I love Louisiana. I own land here and my family and I hunt here. But I started hunting occasionally in Kansas about 15 years ago. My first hunts were for pheasant and quail in north Kansas, along the Nebraska state line. We had great success with the birds. But you know what amazed us? …the size of the whitetail bucks we saw while walking the fields and riding in the area. All we could think about was owning a piece of land in the area. But in the back of our minds we knew it was a long car ride from home…about 14 long, hard hours.

I decided to start searching for property in the southern end of the state. That would shorten my trip to an 8- to 10-hour drive. My thinking was this…I could leave home in Louisiana at 4 AM, make the drive, and I would still have enough time and daylight left to work on stands or possibly hunt on the same day.

In the state of Kansas, the deer limit is one buck per year for resident or nonresident hunters. This factor is one of the reasons there are giant deer killed all over the state each year. If people could kill just one more buck per year – two total – many bucks would never survive long enough to reach trophy potential.

As a nonresident, you are at the mercy of the lottery for your deer tags. You have to choose archery or firearm and hunt that chosen season. There are people who are very successful with this process and do well as nonresident, non-landowner hunters. But they have places to hunt.

Once you have a tag you still have to find a place to hunt. One solution is to lease a piece of property, which can be difficult. Or you can hunt on state-owned walk-on land. I've heard enough stories about hunts gone bad that I don't want to do that! Or you can go with an outfitter. These are several available options for the nonresident hunter…or you can begin to search for a piece of property to own. This is what I like and this is where I can help folks.

In Kansas, if a nonresident owns 80 deeded acres or more he is guaranteed a buck tag every year to hunt on his land. No lottery. No leases. No hassles. You also get to choose your weapon and season. You are able to hunt with a bow or muzzle loader in the early season or rifle hunt in the late season. You are still allowed one buck per year but have more weapons and more time to get him!

I had two partners when we began to look for Kansas hunting property. We wanted 240 acres or more so we could get three 80-acre tags for our tract. In addition to the guaranteed buck tags each year, owning our own property meant we could build a camp, put up permanent stands and be on our own management program. These are big advantages to serious deer hunters. Having more acres by partnering with friends made our management efforts more productive, too.

I want to give you several general things to consider when you decide to look for land in the Midwest. These are things we used in our search for our first Kansas hunting property as well as other bits of information I've learned from listing and selling thousands of acres in Kansas.

Driving distance.

We talked about this a little bit a minute ago, but I want to bring it up again because that drive, depending on where you're coming from, can and will get old. I've seen it get harder and harder each year for people to make that trip. I can introduce you to clients who owned Midwest land and who I have sold hunting property to in north Louisiana and south Arkansas just so they could get back closer to home. Be sure to think through the drive time. Consider the number of days you can actually get away to work on your property, scout, and hunt.

Food, water, & cover.

In the Midwest, food, water, and cover are the most important things to look for when evaluating a possible hunting tract. The term "live water" refers to a river or spring-fed creek. Water is the life source for trees, cover, and all types of game. There are other types of water including ponds, lakes, windmills, and solar-powered wells. If there is sufficient cover for wildlife in these areas where water is available, you might have a place that will hold some giant deer.

Tracts with timber are generally the most desirable. They have the trees for turkeys to roost in and for the deer to hang out in. These wooded areas also provide some relief from the heat in the summer when temperatures rise. It is much cooler in the timber in the heat of the summer, so the game will remain in these areas year-round. Cottonwood, Cedar, Willow and Osage Orange trees are plentiful in these areas. They provide part of the diverse cover needed for wildlife. They also give hunters places to hang stands to hunt for deer!

Cropland planted yearly on the property you plan to purchase is a great help in holding all types of game animals. It will also help keep your animals from wandering onto neighbors' land to search for more food sources.

Good neighbors.

Regardless of what you buy and where you buy it, your chances of success are much better if you can have a neighbor on the same type of management program that you are on. Deer management is a growing practice, and more and more hunters and landowners understand and appreciate the benefits.

I have learned through lots of years of experience that aerial photos and just driving by the tracts on the highway will not tell the whole story about a piece of land. You have to go on each and every acre of the property to evaluate it all as best as you can. You also need to ask around. Talk to adjoining neighbors if you can. Just ask, look, talk, listen, and learn. You'll gather information about the property, the neighbors and the area that can strengthen your decision to buy a particular tract...or warn you to get away as fast as you can!

Mineral rights.

A fourth important factor is mineral rights. Will service companies be driving through the middle of your tract midmorning during the rut? If you own the minerals and have a high-production well, you may not mind the traffic so much. But most of the time these intrusions – as legal and necessary as they are – will just upset you. Especially after that 10-hour drive and if you only have three days to be there! I have seen and experienced these scenarios firsthand. It's my experience that the oil companies will work with you if handled in a reasonable manner. In most cases they will try to do their well-checks in midday during hunting season. It is, however, a real factor that you need to consider.

Owning land and hunting in the Midwest is a dream to many people. They may have bought and sold several tracts in their life where they live, but think that actually owning land "way up yonder" is just not possible. I'm here to tell you that not only is it possible, it could be the beginning of some of the best memories you ever make with family and friends.

Personally, I've learned a lot about buying and selling Midwest land tracts. I've also been able to harvest six bucks with my bow in seven years between 150" and 185". If you are not from the Midwest states and are considering beginning the process of buying land there, I encourage you to go into it with your eyes open, your brain fully engaged, and your goals clearly in mind. Use the short tips I've written here as a starting point. Get a good land agent to help you, and go find your own Midwest sportsman's paradise.

About Jim Rolfe

Jim Rolfe is a licensed professional real estate agent for Brown Realty Company. He is a resident of Oak Ridge, LA and has farmed in Morehouse, Richland, and Ouachita Parishes since 1979. He has experience in cotton, corn, soybeans, and milo. He is an avid hunter and fisherman and loves spending time in the outdoors with his wife and three children Will, Emma, and Mary, who are all avid hunters and fisherman. He has been buying and selling farm and hunting properties since 1990 and is licensed in Louisiana, Mississippi, Arkansas, Oklahoma, and Kansas. You can reach Jim by email at jrolfe@brownrealtyco.com or give him a call at 318-376-5576.

Chapter 3 - Tell Us "What, Why & Where" for the Best Results - By Scott Lindsey

Let's set the stage by listening in to a phone call scenario…

Me: Good morning, United Country Gibson Realty and Land…this is Scott Lindsey.

Caller: Yes, I want to buy some land.

Me: That's great! You called the right place. What type land are you looking for?

Caller: Well, I'd like to get some real pretty land with lots of big pine on it and some hardwoods on it too for the wildlife. I don't want to cut the timber now, but if I ever had to I want it to have enough timber to pay for the land. I like to hunt so I want it to have lots of deer, turkeys, and ducks, too. I think I'd enjoy duck hunting. I don't want it to flood though. I would like a creek on it, something maybe I could fix up as a swimming hole for my kids in the summer. I was thinking maybe 150-200 acres. You think I can get all that for around $50,000?

Me: Sure you can, sir. Call Pat Porter at RecLand Realty. I just don't have time for crazy!

You can't imagine the times in my career as a land broker I have had very similar conversations to the one you just read. Many people want to own land, but they fail to take the necessary steps to ensure they make an informed and educated decision. A decision that could mean the difference between many years of enjoying a smart land investment…or years of struggling to maintain and pay for one.

As a land broker, I'd like to discuss the three main questions that I have potential buyers answer before I start locating potential properties for them to view. I think these are the most important things I need to know to help streamline the process and narrow the options. To me, these answers can make the buying process a lot less stressful on both of us.

WHAT...is your budget?

Yes, I need to get in your business a little bit. I'm not interested in how much you make, how much you have in the bank, or how much Aunt Susie left you in her will. What I do need to know, however, is how much you can afford to pay for the property you're looking for. Are you paying cash? Are you financing? If you are financing, have you applied for a loan? Have you spoken to a loan officer at your bank yet?

Your budget is undoubtedly the single most important factor I need to know in order to help you find precisely what you're looking for. It makes absolutely no sense for me to put a million-dollar property in front of you if can't spend a million dollars. And I don't need to see the properties you can't afford–I've already seen them. Sure, everyone would love to have 1,000 acres with a lake and a cabin (heck, I want that!), and for some it's realistic. But it's not realistic for most. Don't ever be ashamed to tell your agent, "That's a really nice tract. I just can't afford it." I guarantee you any land agent would rather spend time looking at properties in your price range than wasting his and your time in fantasyland.

If you have been saving for years and you plan to pay cash for what you buy, your budget is already established. If you are planning on financing some of your purchase, I encourage you to talk with your lender before starting to look for land. Find out what your options are, what you can afford to borrow, current interest rates, and payment options. Early in my career as a land broker, the lending institutions associated with the Farm Credit System were the most common choice for borrowers. You can check them out at www.farmcreditnetwork.com.

Although these institutions remain a popular choice, I have seen local banks step up their game in the last several years. These local lenders have gotten aggressive in competing for the land market loans they missed out on for so many years. Talk to your agent about lending institutions he has seen other clients have good experiences with.

Let me offer one final suggestion regarding financing. The amount of paperwork you'll be asked to provide as you apply for a loan may seem overwhelming. I do encourage you to shop rates with different lenders, but don't think changing lenders will decrease the document requirements. In the current banking environment, that is just part of the process. I encourage you to find a lending agent and institution with which you feel comfortable and stick it out.

WHY...are you buying this land?

This question isn't nearly as intrusive as the budget question. In most cases it's answered very simply with some of the following responses: "to hunt on," "to fish," "to hang out," "to just get away," "to diversify my investments." As your land broker, I'll need you to be more specific.

Are you expecting a return on this investment? If so, are you expecting an annual return like crop ground provides or are you looking for the long-term return that timber provides? Are you planning on using this property for recreational activities like hunting, fishing, camping, or ATV riding?

Each property is unique in its own way. I need you to be very specific with regards to "why" you want to buy this land. My job is to put the property most suited to your "why" in front of you. In order to do that, I need to know and understand your "why" as thoroughly as possible.

What I have found in many instances is that the "why" sometimes evolves during the looking process. A buyer once told me his "why" was "to have the very best deer hunting property on the market." So I showed this buyer "the very best deer hunting property on the market." He saw that this property was along the Mississippi River and subject to flooding. It had very little timber return. Suddenly his "why" turned into "a good hunting tract where I can still achieve a decent timber return on my investment." Yep…his "why" definitely evolved. As a side note, let me say that the forester in me always likes to see a timber return factored into the "why" of buyers.

The recreational market has grown dramatically over the last 10 years. The "why" of many buyers is simply wanting to have a place for family and friends to enjoy and to just get away. I often hear, "If it's got a few deer that's great. If we see a turkey, great. We just want a place to put a camp and hang out." If that's your "why," let your land agent know. It will make his job much easier, and it will make the most efficient use of your time, too.

WHERE...do you want to buy?

That seems like a really simple question. Most of the time the answer is even simpler: "I don't care as long as I find what I'm looking for." Trust me…that's a terrible answer. The question of "where" has many components.

If you're looking for a timber investment, the "where" opens up a lot of considerations. You should be looking in areas with historically competitive timber prices, pulp and lumber facilities, and reputable logging contractors. The tract you target should have a high site index (be sure to read Rick Taylor's chapter on Site Index), and topography suited for mechanical logging. The ground should have good drainage in order to capitalize on winter timber markets.

The "where" changes again if an agricultural row crop investment is your intent. Your agent should focus on fertile, highly productive farm ground areas. You should be focused on farms with the best tenants and lease rates. In both of these cases, where you buy has nothing to do with where you live. You are simply looking for the best return (see Lannie Philley's chapter on buying farm land for more specifics).

If your desire to buy land focuses on wanting to own a recreational tract, the "where" gets really important. You will have to decide how far you want to drive to reach your property. You'll see that those miles (distance) are worth something. Do you want your land to be 30 minutes from the office for an afternoon hunt? Do you prefer land that is three or more hours from home, and therefore limited to overnight or weekend trips? The use, management, and upkeep on a recreational property takes time with your boots on the ground. It's important for you to factor that time into your decision.

If you're exploring the possibility of buying land, I encourage you first to find a knowledgeable and respected land broker/agent and share with them the answers to the three questions of WHAT – WHY – WHERE before you start your search. You'll both be glad you did.

The final thing I'd like to share with you is something I do for all my clients, buyers and sellers, and something I encourage you to do for yourself and your agent as well.

I found this verse in the Bible in Acts several years ago and it made me take a long hard look at my role as a land broker. Acts 17:26 says, "From one man He made all the nations, that they should inherit the whole earth; and **He fixed himself beforehand the exact times, the boundaries of their land, and the limits of the places where they would live.**"

God already knows the piece of property you'll buy. He knows the boundaries of that property and how long you'll own it. He has been preparing this land for you since before you were born. And during your ownership, He'll be preparing it for the next owner. Understanding this verse helped me to realize my role with clients in buying or selling land. It's not about what I want to sell you. I'm only here to help facilitate God's will.

Remember, he already knows what tract you'll land on. From first contact with a new client, I begin praying that God will show to me the land he has planned for that client. My prayer is that God will allow me to help with his promise that **"…He fixed beforehand the boundaries of their land…"**

Don't get me wrong: I won't ask you to sit around a fire holding hands chanting for the spirits to lead us to the Promised Land. We're just regular folks. In fact, we'll probably end up laughing, spitting, telling stories, and carrying on…and even cuss a little if we walk up on a big moccasin… while we're looking at properties. I am asking you to pray that God will expose the right property to you and that you'll recognize His plan when it's before you.

Good luck and may God bless your land-buying decision.

About Scott Lindsey

Scott Lindsey is a Forester and Broker/Owner of United Country Gibson Realty and Land in McComb, Mississippi. Scott is also the Timberland Director for the United Country Franchise, based out of Kansas City, Missouri. His office has been honored in 8 of the last 9 years as the #1 national office in the United Country Franchise, and in 2010 and 2011 he was the #1 agent in the nation. Scott is a graduate of Mississippi State University School of Forest Resources and has achieved the Accredited Land Consultant designation from the Realtors Land Institute. He has been involved in all aspects of land and timber management since his career began in 1985. The knowledge and experience Scott has gained over the last three decades is something he loves to share with his clients. As a landowner himself, the advice and suggestions Scott has for his clients come from true "boots on the ground" experiences.

Scott lives with his wife Suzanne and their three children, Mary McLean, Jack, and GiGi on their property just outside of McComb, Mississippi. He invites you to contact him anytime at 601-248-3561 or lindseyforestry@hotmail.com.

Chapter 4 - Buying Timberland for Investment and Recreation - By Brandon White

One of the benefits of buying timberland, and just land in general, is that it can offer you a variety of uses. The same acreage that is growing timber as an investment can also be enjoyed recreationally. We'll look at several things to consider when you plan to purchase a tract of land as both a timber investment and a place where you can get away with the family for fun and outdoor enjoyment.

Rick Taylor wrote an excellent chapter on buying timberland as an investment; it focuses on Site Index as a major factor to consider when evaluating different tracts. Be sure you take a look at it. In this chapter, however, I will focus more on the recreational aspects and how timber management weaves its way in as you own, improve, and use the tract.

What is your main priority for the tract?

Decide upfront what you prefer the tract's main strength to be. Do you want a monetary return on timber to be your highest priority? Or is having fun with family and friends the main thing…and making some money on timber just icing on the cake?

By knowing this upfront, your land agent (hopefully you're using a land agent to help you!) can begin to focus his efforts on looking for tracts that fit your top priority. An example of how this can make a difference is the distance a tract is from the mills versus the distance it is from your home. One has big impact on the value of your timber; the other can determine how often you are able to get away and enjoy the tract.

What type of access do you need?

From a timber standpoint, the farther from a good, hard-surfaced access road your property is, the less desirable the timber is to loggers. If your tract is miles down a county dirt road that can get slippery and muddy when wet or dangerously dusty when dry, loggers are not going to be willing to pay as much for your tract as for timber of the same quality along the side of a hard-surfaced road.

But again, if selling timber is not your top priority, then that access will just boil down to your preference. What type roads are you willing to drive on? Do you want to be way off the beaten path? Do you want a quiet and secluded place? Are you willing to drive that same dirt road to have it? Or do you prefer to have something with highway or paved-road access that may be more convenient but less secluded?

Consider the type of road access you have, too. No, not the road's surface and condition we discussed a minute ago, but the road's legal use. Is it a public-access road that anyone can use at any time? It may be an easement that is just for the landowner's (you!) private use. It could also be legally granted to others for their use to cross your property to access their property or to access gas wells, transmission lines, etc. These scenarios are common. Give some thought as to whether you could live with some of these possible situations.

How much time do you have?

"Time" comes into play in a couple different ways. First, growing and managing timber in general is a long-term investment that takes time. Consider how quickly you want or need to see a return on the timber. Do you want to be able to cut timber right away to pay down the note, help with improvements, etc.? Maybe you were planning to use the timber funds to help with college tuition for the kids or grandkids. Answering questions like these will determine whether it's okay to look for tracts with young, pre-merchantable timber that can't be harvested for several more years or whether we need to focus on older, merchantable timber that can be harvested right away.

Now let's look at the factor of time from the recreational use side of it. Do you have the time (and desire) to invest in developing a suitable recreational tract from "scratch"? Establishing roads, trails, shooting lanes, food plots, ponds, camps, and the like is not going to happen overnight. Those things take time, money, and planning.

If you're like me, you'll end up putting a lot more of your time and sweat into it than money. Developing the character of a recreational tract yourself is rewarding. Look at that raw land as a blank canvas. It's yours to do with it what you want however you want.

However, there is another side. If you do not want to invest that time in developing your own recreational property, your land agent will need to look for one that's ready to go. And "ready to go" will mean specific things to each buyer. Finding a tract that has all the required items on the wish list often takes a lot of time.

The money, the timber and the plan.

Obviously, you will most likely pay more for the purchase of a turnkey, ready-to-hunt-or-fish, camp, ride, or a whatever-you-want-to-do property. However, you will most likely spend that same amount of money or more over time to develop the raw land the way you want it. But remember your timber! Your merchantable timber is money on the stump.

One benefit of buying the unimproved timberland is the ability to sell the timber – some or all of it – when you want to or need to. This could help you offset some of the costs of the improvements. Kinda like your own ATM, huh? Well, sort of. There's a lot to it, but yes, you can pull some cash off your land to pay for improvements by selling some timber. But you have to do some planning.

Prior to logging, take the time to plan where you want cabins, shooting lanes, food plots, roads, trails, or ponds. You can then utilize the loggers and their equipment to clear those openings, roads, etc. while they're onsite, as well as get paid for your timber. An added benefit to logging and timber management is that, if done right, it goes hand-in-hand with improving and maintaining a recreational tract.

Don't let that imply you couldn't sell timber off that "turnkey" tract in the same way. You will just have to be a little more particular because those improvements already in place are obstacles to loggers that they will have to work around.

We could have a whole chapter on what to do and how to move forward after the purchase as far as planning, timber sale layouts, and management. I'd encourage you to consult with a forester to help you develop a long-term management plan that fits your goals for the property and can maximize its timber potential.

What type of outdoor recreation are you planning?

Knowing this will help narrow our search down a little more. The recreational opportunities are endless when you consider all the various types of land we have across our great country. I will tell you from my experience in Southeast Texas that some of the biggest recreational pastimes are hunting, fishing, horseback riding, and ATV riding. Like we've already mentioned, the cool thing about it is you can do nearly all of these on the same piece of property that you're growing your timber investment on. With the exception of fishing, the others will pretty much all require the same type of improvements. Let's talk more about hunting and fishing uses, since they are going to require more specific characteristics than just some open trails.

The requirement of a tract that offers fishing is pretty obvious…you have to have water of some sort…a lake, pond, creek, river, or stream on the property. God has taken care of providing the creeks, rivers, and streams. They are already in place and they are where they are.

Lakes and ponds, however, are something you could either build on your property or find on a property that has one already established. A good land agent will be able to help you determine if the topography of a particular tract is potentially suited for capturing enough water to make a lake or pond suitable for your needs. The topography will determine how much or how little dirt work will be needed to make the pond or lake the size you want.

Like fishing, duck hunting requires water here in the south. Most duck species will need some type of open water like a lake, pond, marsh, or slough. Wood ducks are an exception to this. I've seen them in ditches, creeks, streams, and just about anywhere they can fly into a small amount of water. You can hunt them wherever you happen to find them. If you happen to see them there today, chances are they'll be back there in the morning!

If you want to fish or duck hunt, either your land agent will have to key in on tracts with water or you'll need to build money into your budget to create some type of water structure.

The quality of hunting tracts will depend on the type of game you prefer, the habitat on the property you're considering, and the overall amount (acreage) and type of the surrounding habitat that makes up the area your property is in.

The good thing about small game and deer is that you can control the numbers and quality to a large degree. Improving the habitat can start making a significant change in the wildlife within a year or two on most tracts. Believe it or not, timber management is a major contributor to wildlife habitat improvement.

There are three basic habitat components that nearly all wildlife, especially whitetail deer, need in order to thrive: they are cover, food, and water. Although having natural water on the property is a plus, it's not a necessity. But if there's a drought and your neighbor has a creek on his tract, then that's where most of the wildlife will be.

Ideally, you want to find a property with all three components. A tract with natural water or a pond, hardwoods for mast production, openings for browse and herbaceous forbes and thick cover for shelter and protection is ideal. Having this diversity is the key and a best-case scenario. If one or more of those components are missing, however, with time and money you can establish it through supplemental feeding, planting, watering, etc.

So whether all the components are there or you have to create a few, they are beneficial for all sorts of wildlife and worth your efforts and money to try to enhance them as you're able. Developing the overall habitat is a worthwhile project whether you're in it for the hunting, just watching and enjoying the wildlife, or some of both. Again, like previously discussed, just the way logging and timber management can positively change and manipulate the habitat tremendously benefits wildlife.

There are many resources available to landowners to provide guidance for wildlife habitat improvement. A few sources we use and support are www.qdma.com, www.nwtf.com, and www.ducks.org.

To me, the pros of owning and managing land for timber and recreation far outweigh all the negatives. Being able to take the friends, family, kids, and grandkids out to a place they can get around on, see, feel, explore, and really experience nature is humbling to say the least. The memories made and the legacy left can be priceless.

I know we've looked at a lot of things here in general terms. Detailed information on each of the factors we've talked about is readily available by talking with professional land managers, land agents, foresters, and wildlife specialists. The main thing I'd like you to take away from this is to be aware that thinking through these factors now – even before you have in-depth information on them – can help you focus your time on finding and buying the property that best fits your needs and priorities. Actually knowing what your "dream property" is will make it much easier to find.

About Brandon White

Brandon White is a Forester and an Associate Broker with RecLand Realty in Texas and Louisiana. He lives with his family in Jasper, Texas. His forestry career has taken him to both the corporate and private side of forestry. Jobs have ranged from logging and procurement management for Louisiana Pacific, to managing approximately 50,000 acres for Rice University in Louisiana, to small, non-industrial private land management and consulting. Brandon has been in real estate off and on since 2000 and has been a full time land agent since 2012. He has a passion for wildlife and the outdoors and is happy to share that passion with whoever will listen.

Brandon can be reached at hbwhite55@gmail.com. His listings are at www.recland.net.

Chapter 5 - Due Diligence – Some Additional Items to Check Before Buying Rural Land - By Pat Porter

I looked up the definition of due diligence in several places and found these recurring words: investigation, analysis, research, reasonable, certainty, and confirmation. These are heavy words that carry a lot of responsibility. And all this responsibility falls squarely on the shoulders of you, dear buyer, when you plan to buy land.

No one will care about the details of the deal more than you. Doing your due diligence can save you a lot of future heartache and money on that land tract you're about to buy. In this short chapter, I'll outline several key areas, in addition to the usual things most people check when buying real estate, that will get you thinking about what else to check and verify before your next rural real estate purchase.

The Purchase Contract

Due diligence starts with the purchase contract. Read it, understand it, ask questions about it, and use it to fully detail the terms of the purchase as they have been negotiated with the seller. Your land agent should be diligent to help you document the terms of the deal clearly in the purchase contract. Having the seller and buyer see "eye to eye" on the terms at this stage of the deal will reduce the chances of something going wrong for either party before closing. Regardless of how well things seem to be going at this stage, get all the verbal agreements written into the contract. Even the best of intentions can fall prey to bad memories and misunderstandings later on.

Remember that by design, a purchase contract will capture all the big items in a deal that rarely cause problems. Things like purchase price, closing date, and legal descriptions won't usually be an issue later on. It's the smaller things that creep up and bugger up a deal (yea, "bugger up" is a technical real estate term!) Get those smaller details on paper at the beginning.

Existing Easements & Leases

Depending on the present use of the land, you will need to verify a number of items that will affect your future use of the tract. Have you seen the CRP or WRP contracts that are still in place on the tract? Have you read the restrictions of the conservation easement, the deed restrictions, timber reservations, or other encumbrances that will limit the use of the tract? Have you or your attorney actually seen and read them? What about that hunting lease or farm lease…does it match what you were told during the negotiating process? Ask to see the conveyance document on "deeded accesses" if you are depending on it for your supposed legal access.

All the above contracts and leases are available either as recorded documents in your county or parish records (these are public information), the local Farm Service Agency (you'll need the land owner's permission to get copies) or from the current owner. Be sure your written purchase agreement has language that says the seller has provided you with a copy of any lease, easement, or agreement that may not be found in the public records.

Here's an example of how this type of follow-up saved a large acreage deal. I was helping a group of buyers purchase nearly 2,000 acres of bottomland that was a purely recreational tract. They knew they weren't getting the mineral rights since those rights were already under lease and the tract had a number of producing gas wells on it. They were concerned, however, that all the coming and going of the gas company would be a problem for them when trying to divide the tract and sell parcels to hunters. After all, who wants to spend a bunch of money on a place to deer hunt and then have people riding through your property at 9 AM checking on a gas well?

I found out who the gas company was and made a call. I was able to speak with the field supervisor for that area and that tract. He told me they had a policy about limiting property visits during hunting season and that they try to come only during the middle of the day when a visit was necessary.

This piece of information eased the buyers' minds and they bought the tract. Their resell efforts were also successful since this little bit of information was enough to make the original concern a nonissue. But they wouldn't have known without the additional phone call. And it's the kind of phone call and follow up that isn't part of the closing attorney's general checklist of things to do. You have to do this for yourself.

Wetlands

If you plan to clear some of the tract for farming, development, or even a new road, will you be clearing wetlands? You don't know until you've seen a wetland determination report. Will that bridge you need require a 404 Permit from the Corps of Engineers or expensive mitigation credits?

Go to the Corps website at www.usace.army.mil and click on the link "Find a Corp Office" to get the office in your area. You'll find there are 30-40 offices in the United States, with most of them located in the eastern half of the country. Call and ask if you're not certain.

"But Pat, I'll be opening up a can of worms if I call them!" I hear you…and tend to agree a little bit. But you could be opening a can of snakes – in the form of expensive litigation and after-the-fact remedies – if you don't check before you begin an expensive or expansive project. Our experience has shown that these folks will just guide you to perform only what's necessary as your project impacts wetlands, streams, etc. and leave you alone if your plans don't otherwise cross into this type of problem areas.

If in doubt…call them before you buy.

Environmental Issues

Diligent buyers of farmland look for large diesel spills at wells and near full tanks and check for empty chemical containers dumped in nearby ditches or creeks to alert them of potential environmental quality issues. A Phase 1 environmental evaluation is not a big deal to get, but it could turn into a big deal if you don't.

You can get good information about this from your state's Department of Environmental Quality. Simply Google "Department of Environmental Quality" to find your state's particular website.

Timber Markets

Timberland buyers should understand the area markets and mills if buying a tract in a new area. How far away are the area mills and what type of wood product are they taking? Will the terrain allow a complete mechanical harvest, or are there acres that loggers just won't be able to work? This can be a costly thing to find out later if you put a considerable value on the timber in those unworkable areas. Do you have good access to get your timber out? Not all timber markets are the same. Not all timber tracts are the same, either. Consulting a local forester in an area you're new to may prevent a costly mistake.

Title, Mineral, and Groundwater Checks

Your closing attorney should be able to catch title issues that may cause you problems if left unresolved, but you may need to specify that he look for items that are critical to your reason for purchase. For instance, if you're buying half the mineral rights, does that mean half of 100%, or does the seller only own 50% herself and you're really just getting half of half? A general title search will not necessarily determine this information for you. If confirming this information is critical, you'll need to take the initiative to have a mineral abstract performed.

Just a word of caution about title searches. It could be helpful to you to be sure your attorney checks the title back further than a typical "30 years plus 1 chain" in order to pick up some old leases that may have been executed 40, 50 years ago or more. These leases exist. I've seen them and I've seen this very issue create problems for buyers and sellers. A title policy can help reduce risks associated with title issues. We have a chapter devoted to title policies in this book. It's written by a practicing attorney who specializes in real estate transactions. Be sure to read it.

If you are buying land in a state like Texas where groundwater can be reserved, you will want to know the status of your tract. Be sure to ask your attorney or title company.

Flood Plains and Access to River Tracts

You can verify river stages, flood histories, and FEMA flood plain data yourself if the tract is in a marginal elevation area. But *you* need to do this. Ask your land agent to help you identify internet resources if you need them. Confirm the information you've been told if you're unsure. Ask your homeowner's insurance agent to help you check the area where you may plan to build a home or a camp.

At what river stage at the nearest upstream bridge does a rising river cut off use of the access road to your property? When was the last time it got this high…or how often?

Here's the best place to start if you want to investigate the federal database for floodplains in the US. Go to www.fema.gov. Click the Navigation tab on the left. Scroll down and click the Flood Map Service Center tab. This will take you to a page where you can enter the property's location and the site will locate the flood plain map for that area. You'll see an overview of the flood zone designations. This is a good place to start, especially if you have plans to build on the property.

The list of items to verify can go on and on depending on the tract and its use. The point is to confirm, verify, and understand all the major items that will impact you the most. Your land agent is required by law to tell you about all material facts he is aware of that may impact the property's value and use. The key is "that he is aware of." Your agent may not know everything about every detail that is critical to you. You as the buyer are ultimately responsible to satisfy and protect your future interests, to your satisfaction and level of comfort, with thoughtful due diligence.

About Pat Porter

Pat Porter is the broker for RecLand Realty, LLC. His company site is www.RecLand.net and its video blog is www.RecLandTalks.com.

Feel free to email Pat at patlporter@bellsouth.net. See the end of the book for details.

Chapter 6 - Buy or Pass: What to Look for When Buying Farm Land - By Lannie B. Philley

A young rancher's son once questioned his father about their cattle business by asking, "Why do we continue in the cow business?" His wise father answered, "Son, you buy cattle when you got money and you sell cattle when you need money!" Ironically, this is sometimes the approach of land buyers.

As someone who has been in the land management business for thirty-one years in both the selling and buying of farm properties, I have seen many different approaches to buying or selling a property. My business has been more focused on the buying side than the selling side by a ratio of 9 to 1. I am a licensed real estate broker, and that side of me is heavily weighted by laws, rules, and regulations that all brokers must live by.

In the next few pages, I will attempt to steer away from the brokerage side of the transaction and concentrate on how I approach buying a ranch, recreational property, or commodity-producing farm. I will also illustrate the different buying strategies of an individual buyer, a single investment buyer, an institutional buyer, or my own personal purchases. Each of these types of buyers has different driving forces for a purchase. These differences can consist of available funds, future and current expansions, rate of return, inheritance plans, investment diversification, crop diversification, and pride of ownership or retirement.

While these differences are inherently primary, there are many secondary forces – such as interest rates, commodity market prices, strength and weakness of the dollar, government regulations, uncertainty in the stock market, and a lack of alternative investments – that will weigh on the buyer. I will address each buyer from my point of view as if I were buying for them. I will also address the most important assets of a property that I look for in the initial analysis.

At this point, I must be honest with you in disclosing that I also manage all properties that I buy for a client, with the exception of the individual buyer who may happen to be an owner-operator who operates his purchase as he wishes. Therefore, I am likely more conservative in my purchases than most. In several purchases, I have actually bought farms for clients sight-unseen by the buyer. So as you can see, if I give the recommendation to buy, I have much to lose.

There are seven important assets of a property to me, which I will give to you in order of importance. They are drainage, availability of quality tenants, proximity of commodity storage and processing, soil quality, available water, real estate taxes, and access. Let's take a look at each one.

Drainage

Drainage must be first and foremost. This includes recreational properties or ranches, because poor drainage will kill timber or impede grass production. You can't start to improve a property until you drain it. It is wasted money to try. Good drainage improves everything. I can cite over twenty purchases that I have seen where a property has all of the assets I look for except drainage. Time and time again, these properties promise everything; but in the end they fall short on yields or completely lose a crop and all meaningful income. On the flip side, I have seen farms with excellent drainage but poor soil quality and good access perform well as investment-grade properties. If it lacks good drainage, walk away.

Tenant Availability

I gave a speech not long ago, and during the question and answer session at the end, an investor asked me what makes a good farm manager. I told him picking the right tenant. I know that I am right, and after thirty-one years of experience-giving proof…I'm convinced.

The availability of quality tenants gives strength and protection to a property. It also provides the climate of competition that is essential in tenant-landowner negotiations. In addition, it lowers repair and maintenance costs, which can be the biggest expense in the operating budget of a landowner. A quality tenant can and will give a manager and landowner the best advice of anyone because he is on the property more than anyone. He has the ability to see firsthand all the little things that could enhance the yields or value of the property. A quality tenant can also save the manager time and money because when he calls about a problem, he can relay the problem in meaningful, clear language that the manager can depend on.

A very good example of the importance of good tenants is in an area of an adjoining state to mine. It has some of the best soil and water in the state, but lacks available quality tenants. Consequently, this area suffers in land prices. Likewise, there are inferior soil types and other issues in areas that enjoy excellent rent and value numbers simply because of the abundance of quality tenants and the competition among them to lease the available farms.

Commodity Storage and Processing

A farm can produce excellent yields, but if there are extraneous costs associated with storage and/or processing the crops, guess what? That's right. The land value will suffer. It will suffer not just from the absence of this asset but also because it will fail to attract the quality tenants we just discussed. This same area in an adjoining state that I mentioned in the previous paragraph also suffers from a lack of storage facilities, ginning capabilities, and commodity buyers.

I currently manage a farm for some foreign owners that proves this point. Normal trucking costs for corn and soybeans of $.15 to $.30 per bushel are $.50 to $1.00 per bushel for this farm because of no local storage facilities. Yes, a landowner can build on-farm storage, but he will still incur trucking charges for that grain. This important asset is often overlooked more than any, but it is essential in the evaluation process. Land sales in these areas support my opinion that this factor plays a big role in market values.

Soil Quality

I once had the advantage of working as an agricultural lender for a bank. One of the major stockholders in the bank, who was a landowner and farmer, told me that you can't pay too much for quality soil. In many ways, he was right. Soil quality makes up for lots of mistakes. But it can also hide poor performance by a tenant. My grandfather told me, "Son, you can't win the Kentucky Derby on a Jack Ass." Ha! He was right, too.

It is still true. Soil quality is critical, but technology, new farming practices, etc. have narrowed the difference between Class III soils and Class I soils. I must be honest here and point out that the tenant must be included in any discussion of the performance of Class III soils versus Class I soils.

Here's what I mean: assuming the tenants are comparable, I have hard facts supporting 197 bushel corn on Sharkey Clay (a Class III soil) and 197 bushel corn on Commerce Silt Loam (a Class I soil) with both being furrow irrigated. This was the case even though there are three main advantages of Class I Silt Loam over Class III clay soils. The first is drainage that facilitates a timely harvest. The second is nutrient requirements. A third advantage is workability. Normally, an operator can get into the field much faster in Class I soils versus Class III.

Available Water

Because the profit margins are narrowing in farm operations, financially stable tenants are decreasing. Therefore, more and more lenders are looking for operators with irrigated farms. This illustrates my point about available water. A case in point is the high plains of Texas, parts of Arizona, and especially California. Land values in the high plains have decreased substantially because of the falling water table. In Arizona, a farm with irrigation separated by a mere thirty-foot road from a farm without irrigation can have a difference in value of $5,000 per acre. I am presently seeing tenants not being able to obtain financing because of lack of irrigation. I also don't have any clients buying non-irrigated cropland unless it has good groundwater or available surface water that can be developed. If you're buying a farm, it must have water.

Real Estate Taxes

Real estate taxes are becoming a real problem. When I prepare a landowner budget for a purchase, there is a real difference in $2.75-per-acre taxes and $10.75-per-acre. On a 5,000-acre farm this equates to $40,000. That difference in taxes is the cost of leveling and watering 80 acres of cropland, or the cost of two turbine irrigation wells.

I now have some investors advising me not to try to buy farms in some areas due to taxes. And if I do, the offer I make to the owner will be less than comparable areas simply because of the added tax burden. This problem is going to get worse as municipalities and counties lose taxpayers. Also, when the majority of taxpayers don't own land and therefore don't pay any real estate taxes, it's really easy for them to vote to increase the property taxes on those of us who do own land.

Access

Access, of course, is essential; but quality access can and does make a difference to me as a buyer. There is some difference in a property adjacent to a gravel road as opposed to a blacktop highway. There is a difference in a prime property located within ten miles of a town and one located twenty-five miles from the nearest town – all else being equal. As a personal buyer, it doesn't make much difference to me, but it does to most buyers. You'll have to decide what you prefer regarding quality of access and make your decisions accordingly.

These are the seven critical assets that I look at closely on any farm I'm considering buying.

Now let's take a look at the four types of buyers I represent, and the differences of each.

Owner-operator Buyer

There are major differences in what I look for depending on the type of buyer I'm buying for. I don't represent many individual buyers who intend to operate the farms themselves. I have only one client in this classification. He is hard to deal with because his reason for buying can vary greatly, and he might ask me to find something in just two weeks. This is not easy! He may buy for any number of reasons:

To enhance his other income assets, such as grain facilities.

Or…to take advantage of an IRS 1031 exchange.

Or…because he is selling a property that is located a great distance from his home and wants to consolidate his assets closer to home.

He is a bargain hunter and a wholesale buyer. This owner-operator looks first at what this purchase will add to his organization.

Buyers who are owner-operators have different calculations in their cash flows than other types of buyers – and that is a whole different subject! The point is, each purchase for an owner-operator can be motivated by a number of factors. If you're this type of buyer, it's important that you clearly identify the major motivating factor and communicate that to the land agent, who may be helping you try to find the farm that is right for you. This clarity will bring some focus that can save everyone a lot of time.

Single Investment Buyer

I represent several single investment buyers. These buyers are very interesting, to say the least. This type of buyer differs from the owner-operator in that he doesn't farm the tract himself. He will be looking for the quality tenant we discussed earlier. This buyer gets his return on a farm from the annual lease or crop-share payments he gets from the tenant. He will also gain value from the asset as it appreciates over time and/or from improvements made.

One particular buyer I represent will not look at anything except Class I silt loam farms that grow cotton, corn, and soybeans. The other assets of the farm don't matter. He doesn't want to make any major improvements. When I buy for him, I am looking for Class I soils, excellent access, and water. He likes it completely turn-key and ready to operate at full potential from day one.

Another one of my clients gives me a different approach. He prefers Class III soils for rice and soybeans and preferably surface water. Development is big on his list, and he doesn't mind the expense. He enjoys the input of his own design and gets great pleasure in taking a $2,500-per-acre farm and making it into a $4,000-per-acre farm. He does own several Class I farms, but his reasoning for those is to balance his portfolio for his children and decrease his risk exposure to one type of crop. I like his approach.

Institutional Investment Buyer

Chances are you're reading this book as a single investment buyer and not as an institutional buyer. This type of buyer is interesting, and more and more farms are being bought for larger investment portfolios, so let's take a look at what they require.

An institutional buyer has several limitations on what he wants and what he's allowed to buy. Diversification of his portfolio is paramount. Secondly, concentration is very important. Third, access and location are high on his list. After I address these three criteria, I apply my seven most important assets to the search. You remember those? Drainage, tenants, commodity storage, etc.? Yea, you remember.

The institutional buyer may also be limited in the amount of capital improvements he is allowed to perform. For example, I have one client who is limited to 10% of the purchase price for capital improvements. Retirement funds regulated by the SEC are more regulated than just an investment fund. There can be wide variations in the guidelines we have to follow for each type fund.

Diversification for a fund means the portfolio would need to consist of row crops such as corn, soybeans, cotton, etc., produce such as asparagus, sweet peas, potatoes, and citrus, and maybe table grapes or a wine vineyard. Concentration limits the amount of each type of product in each area of the country. For example, one fund with a $100 million portfolio may limit $25 million to the Delta, $25 million to the Midwest, $25 million to the West, and $25 million to the Southeast United States. It also means the investor does not want all $100 million in corn and soybeans.

The institutional buyer wants a large tract as a unit, not five different tracts of one farm. They want it to be visible and highly attractive. One of the reasons for this in my opinion is that should liquidity be needed, it is much easier to sell a portfolio of farms if they all have this feature.

Myself as a Buyer

"Ok," you say, "You buy for others…how do you look at deals for yourself?" Well, as for myself as a buyer, I try to apply all of the items that I have mentioned in this chapter. But personally, I will not be as hard on some of these as I would be for an investor. The two criteria that I apply first are available funds and rate of return. I then look at drainage and available quality tenants because I want people calling me to rent my land. I don't have time to be looking for tenants, and neither will my children, who this investment is really for anyway.

In summary, I take the approach of agricultural purchases differently than most real estate brokers. My vision for a purchase is long-term, period. It is no different than my personal investments in the stock market, which are "Blue Chip" companies with decent dividends. Buy and hold. I don't represent buyers who are land traders. It doesn't fit my program or organization.

Regardless of the type of buyer you are, based on the thousands of acres of farmland I've evaluated and helped buy, you'll do well to apply the criteria I've outlined here to your farmland purchase.

About Lannie B. Philley

Lannie B. Philley is the land manager for Delta Land & Farm Management, Co. LLC located in Mer Rouge, LA. He spends his time managing agricultural property for absentee landowners. In addition to land management, he purchases agricultural property for several clients. He can be reached at his office in Mer Rouge, LA at 318-647-5744 or email at lbp@dlfmllc.com.

Chapter 7 - Developing Rural Land for Residential Uses - By Rockland Burks

For several years, I have been active in the rural land and timber business. I have represented both buyers and sellers in tens of thousands of acres of land transactions. I have seen a few great deals come across my desk, as well as some really bad ones. I have participated in both, unfortunately, but have all the while been learning from each one.

Most deals are fairly simple. You have two motivated parties (buyer and seller), they have agreed on a sales price, lawyers are hired, title is checked, due diligence on the part of the buyer is performed (see Pat's excellent chapter on this), loan papers are approved, and the deal is signed. The buyer now owns the land and the seller moves on with his cash.

There are several reasons land sales occur. In the south, inheritance creates a lot of land sales. Normally the 1st generation acquires the land, 2nd generation inherits, holds, and maintains the land, and the 3rd generation inherits, sells, and turns the land to cash. Another reason land trades hands is a changing lifestyle. Property that was once a great hunting tract when the kids were young is now harder to maintain when they're grown and gone. People also upgrade investment land to bigger tracts, more convenient locations, or a tract with a more diversified or more valuable use.

The key to knowing the difference between a good deal and a bad deal is being educated in local markets well enough to have a good instinct in knowing a good deal when you see one. This instinct is honed by experience. It's rare to see someone young without experience make a lot of good deals. They may make a few good ones, but normally they make a few bad ones, too. And it's the bad ones that can undo all the financial progress gained by the earlier good ones.

As mentioned, I have represented many clients buying and selling rural timber lands. I have also bought and sold many tracts myself…individually and with partners. I have seen investors purchase rural land for multiple purposes. The most common reason for purchases is for recreational and long-term timberland growth. While this can provide a sustained long-term appreciation on their investment, it typically does not produce a quick return. Timber takes time to grow. It does not produce a realized annual return like most agricultural crops or rental properties. Timber harvests normally occur every 8 to 15 years. This is a long wait for investors wanting cash flow returns on a steady basis.

Developing rural land for residential uses can be another investment alternative for investors wanting a faster return. Time can vary as to how long the investment will take to produce a return and is dependent on many factors.

The following are some of the most important factors to consider when buying property for rural land development.

Size of the parent property.

The size of the property has to do with the size of the acreage. This will determine how many units you may be able to develop out of the parent property for resale. The parent property is the tract that you are subdividing into lots or smaller tracts.

The absorption rate.

The absorption rate has to do with the amount of potential capable, willing buyers there are in the local market. You may ask, "How do I determine this?" Good question! My advice would be to drive around the area where you are planning to purchase and see how much land is for sale. Make notes of where the available lots are, numbers still for sale, current construction taking place in new subdivisions, and new infrastructure development occurring in the general area. The infrastructure development can be an indication of planned, long-term residential growth in the area.

Call local Realtors who have land listed and get all the information they are willing to share. Always try to get the number of days on the market of comparable lots that are for sale. If you are finding that most of the current listed property has been for sale for an average of 180 days or more, then the absorption rate for that area is very low. If the opposite is true, this area may have more room for quick returns on residential development lots. Areas with high absorption rates are where you want to purchase land for rural development.

Location of the parent property.

I can't believe I'm about to write this old real estate cliché in a no-cliché land book…but it's true, so here it is: Location, Location, Location. Location is a major factor in developing rural land.

I have seen distances of less than a mile play a critical role in how quickly a development sells. A good investor always looks for the "come." The "come" is the area where people are moving to, building, or want to be moving to and building. Knowing these locations before everyone else is part of that instinct I talked about earlier. Instinct comes from informed – or educated – assumptions. Know your market and investment areas. Pay attention to what's going on around you and what people are doing, saying, and spending their money on. Learn to identify the up-and-coming areas of growth.

Public utilities availability.

This is hands-down one of the most important factors in deciding whether or not to proceed with buying a large tract for development. Remember, in rural land development you want to be ahead of the "come." Unfortunately, being ahead of the "come" sometimes puts you behind the infrastructure of the local utilities.

Always check with local utilities to see if they have service in the area and the capabilities to support the development you are planning. Just seeing water service nearby doesn't guarantee that your project can be serviced. Many times, water companies will see your development as an opportunity to get a portion of their inadequate system upgraded…and on your dime! I, along with partners and friends in other development projects, have had this battle numerous times. Do we spend a ton of money to upgrade the water lines for a half-mile to service our tract, or is it just too much money to allow the project to be profitable?

Electricity is no given, either, just because you see poles nearby. Who is the electric company, and what are their requirements for new service? Will they need a large, upfront capital expenditure from you to run service? Will some or all of this expense be refunded to the developer as lots are sold, or as homes are built and permanent customers are being served, or at all? How long do they allow for any refunds to given to the developer? No two electric companies are quite the same. Each has their own requirements. Ask. Check. Find out.

A lack of utilities is a major problem when developing rural land. The cost of running utilities to your property may be so expensive that it prevents you from doing your project.

Elevation.

Determine if your property is in a flood zone. Flood prone property is not always black and white. It can be confusing. There are two types of flood zones: flood zone A and flood zone X. Flood zone A is generally a low-lying area with some type of water body flowing through it. This area is easy to see, and common sense knows not to build in it.

Zone X can be tricky. This is an area where backwater can flow into and flood. Heavy rains with historic rainfall amounts recently flooded several subdivisions in my area. Water from area creeks, bayous, and rivers backed up into zone X and flooded many homes in what are normally high-and-dry subdivisions. Consulting a surveyor or engineer can give you more detailed information regarding flood potential.

The local red tape.

You will have some local, county or parish, municipal, or some other legally recognized body of jurisdiction that will regulate just about any type development you choose to pursue. There is really no way to get around this. And the harder you try to get around it, the more money you'll spend correcting your issues…or just scrapping your project all together.

While these governing bodies are more often than not a pain to deal with, they do have a place and do provide a service for the common good. So let's find a way to make our work with them a smoother process.

This book is not the place to detail, or even outline, the steps to navigate your local governing bodies. The myriad of details will vary dramatically from area to area…even from town to town in the same areas. But there are a couple of common threads I'll mention to get you started down the right road.

   a. Get a copy of the subdivision ordinances that apply to your location. These will be available online or by making a phone call to a local engineer, surveyor, or attorney you know who has developer clients.

b. While you're talking to an engineer or surveyor about getting the subdivision ordinances, start a conversation to interview them for your project. You'll need their services to develop plans and plats for your project. Ask around before you make a commitment to an engineer and a surveyor. These services are both critical and costly, so you'll want real pros who know how to navigate the local system with professional work. Find out if they deliver their work in a timely manner and if they are good at keeping you posted on where things stand. There is nothing worse in this business than being at the mercy of third parties who will not keep you posted on progress, timetables, issues, etc. It's your time and your money at stake.

c. Have a good attorney who can help you with the legal details that arise, such as Home Owner's Associations, liability issues, getting your final plans approved, public road dedications, access issues, deed restrictions and covenants, and on and on and on. As with above…be sure to ask around before you commit to their services.

d. Have the mindset to spend your time following the ordinances, not trying to get around them. You'll usually spend less money doing it right…as long as you have a good team (engineer, surveyor, and attorney) helping you. The time and money it takes to go back and correct your shortcut can destroy the profits in a deal.

I have given you six broad-brush factors to determine if the property you have is ideal for development. There are many smaller details that must not be overlooked, but these are the key factors that make the foundation of a good rural development deal.

Simply put, developing rural land is an educated gamble. But heck…just about any business venture is. Play your cards right, and it can produce a sound return on your investment.

About Rockland (Rocky) Burks

Rockland R. Burks (RRB) is a registered forester in Arkansas and Mississippi. RRB is also a licensed real estate broker in Arkansas and Louisiana. RRB graduated with a forestry degree from the University of Arkansas Monticello in May of 1999. He has worked in both the private and corporate sides of the forestry business and has been active in the real estate business since 1999. RRB currently owns and manages Rockland R. Burks Inc., a forestry company that works in the land and timber business. In the last five years, RRB has developed several rural tracts of land into multi-unit residential units and is still active in this market. RRB can be reached at rocky@rrbland.com.

Chapter 8 - Do I Need to Buy Owner's Title Insurance When Buying Rural Property? - By Paul Hurd

As you will surmise, I am an owner of a title company that conducts closings of real estate transactions: acquisitions and refinancing. Because of my business and the fellowship arising in informal social settings, I am often asked about the wisdom of buying Owner's Title Insurance in conjunction with the purchase of a piece of real property.

Before I tell you how I answer that question, let me say that this chapter will address "Owner's Title Insurance" for the protection of the Buyer(s) of a purchased tract of real property. For ease of reference, this title coverage will be referred to as "Title Insurance." The issues concerning "Lender's Title Insurance" relate purely to the underwriting requirements of the Buyer's lender if the Buyer borrows some or all of the purchase money funds and the lender requires that the acquired real property be used as collateral for the Buyer's loan. If the property is being acquired without anticipation of substantial improvements and appreciation of value related thereto, it is likely that the acquisition of the Owner's Title Insurance and the Lender's Title Insurance is much less expensive if done at the initial acquisition and initial borrowing.

Back to that question. I usually answer it with my own cocktail party response:

"How much MONEY are you spending, and will you mind losing it?

AND

"Do you know what 'MERCHANTABLE TITLE' is, and are you getting it?"

With these two compound questions, a prospective Buyer of a new tract of property can focus on the very real financial issues that must be evaluated to determine whether the Buyer's financial circumstances justify the purchase of Owner's Title Insurance when the real property is purchased. For purposes of this essay on title insurance issues, I will presume that the typical prospective Buyer will have answered my cocktail questions like this:

> "A darn good bit and Heck No!" AND "I don't know and I don't know."

Following this usual response, the odds are better than 3 to 1 that the next question from the prospective Buyer's mouth will be: "Do you need a fresh drink?" My usual answer, if I am not too thirsty is: "No, but you probably need to buy that Title Insurance when you do the deal!"

In the world of prospective Buyers of real estate, it is wise to rely on the local knowledge and expertise (and the recommendations) of the Buyer's own retained title attorney, title company or real estate broker to determine whether the prospective Buyer expects to have "Merchantable Title" when the property is purchased, without any exceptions that interfere with the use of the property by the Buyer. Normally, the purchase of real property means the Buyer is seeking "Merchantable Title" of the property from a legal standpoint. Nonetheless, your own home study of "Merchantable Title" and "Title Insurance" coverages – including reviewing this book and this chapter – will better prepare you to confidently determine whether to buy the property and the associated "Title Insurance" or to be comfortable taking the financial risk associated with not purchasing it.

Let's look at this in more detail.

What is a "Title Opinion" and "Owner's Title Insurance?"

Owner's Title Insurance is an insurance product that insures the Owner of real estate (the insured) against a claim that the Owner does not have "Merchantable Title" on the real estate that is the subject of the Title Insurance.

The American Land Title Association has established standard title insurance policies, and standard exceptions therein, that are functional and accepted in the real estate and banking businesses. Generally, the standard exceptions to the Owner's Title Policy can be eliminated with an endorsement and investigatory actions taken before the purchase. An overview of the coverage of owner's title policies and the usual exceptions can be accessed on the internet through the American Land Title Association website: www.alta.org.

In the past, this third-party guaranty to a Buyer that the Buyer is getting "Merchantable Title" came from the "Title Opinion" given by a local attorney. With the ever-growing regulations heaped on federally insured lenders, for any large loan (above $100,000 or above $250,000), the financial institutions require Title Insurance instead of a Title Opinion. The difference to the lender is that the title insurance companies never die (though the lawyers doing the title opinions do!), never retire (lawyers hope to) and the title company has a substantial net worth (attorneys just hope to). For the lender, the regulations have moved the title industry into the Title Insurance business.

As for the "Title Insurance" business, Title Insurance has evolved into insurance that protects a Buyer from the financial losses that arise if title-insured property turns out not to have Merchantable Title. This product provides three primary benefits to the Owner.

First, if a third-party challenges your ownership of the insured title, the Title Insurance Company will pay the survey, court, and defense costs that arise to assert that the insured Owner does have Merchantable Title. Second, the Title Insurance Company will pay the expenses incurred to correct the title defect or to acquire the interest from the third-party. Third, if the title defect is real and it cannot be eliminated or cured, the Title Insurance Company will pay the insured Owner for the damage to the property up to the insured amount on the policy. In substance, the Title Insurance protects the insured Owner's financial investment in the insured parcel so a title defect, undiscoverable by the Buyer, does not cause significant financial damage to the Buyer.

What is "Warranty of Title" and "Merchantable Title" in Different States?

A. The Traditional "Warranty Deed."

To discuss "Merchantable Title", it is best to know a little bit about the "usual" terms, representations, and warranties that are included in a "Warranty Deed" from a seller to a buyer of real property in the particular State.

The basic "Warranty Deed" will warrant the title of the property, and also warrant the physical condition of improvements on the subject property. These warranties concerning the physical condition of the improvements, or their relative usefulness for intended purposes, do not usually arise as an important issue in buying larger tracts of rural property, as the improvements are not the focus of the financial value of the property. However, if the rural tract also includes a valuable improvement (camps, homes, irrigation systems, warehouses, etc.), the warranty as to the physical condition of the improvements becomes an independent issue that is addressed by retaining skilled inspectors (engineers, construction contractors, etc.) to review the condition of the improvements included in the property.

The "warranty" provisions within the "Warranty Deed" are affirmative representations by the Seller that are enforceable against the Seller after the sale of the real estate if the warranty is legally incorrect. These warranty provisions make the Seller financially liable if the warranty is incorrect. For example, if the Seller warrants merchantable title, and there is a large pipeline down the middle of the property that prevents its use, the Seller will be liable for the damages, or depending on the state might be forced to purchase the property back.

The inclusion or exclusion of these various "warranty" items and their coverage is different in different states. Remember, the "warranty" is just a promise to pay if the Seller is wrong, and is an unsecured right to sue. Because Sellers want their risk associated with the sale to end with the sale, many Sellers no longer want to include a full warranty on a sale. It is standard commercial practice for Sellers to negotiate a sale with a limited warranty or without warranty. This occurs with Sellers of large properties, including rural properties, depending on the sophistication and financial strength (or arrogance) of the large tract seller. Nonetheless, the basic "Warranty Deed" will warrant from the Seller to the Buyer the following:

1. The Seller has "Merchantable Title" to the property;

2. The property includes ownership of surface rights and surface water rights;

3. There are no use restrictions or building limitations, burdening servitudes, or surface rights of way on the property;

4. The property has a functional connection to a public road, or to and through a private right of ingress and egress from the property to a public road; and

5. The property is free and clear of all mortgages, liens, or encumbrances (except Buyer's own).

It is worth repeating that the warranty of Merchantable Title by the Seller only gives the Buyer the right to sue the Seller if the warranties are not correct, and provides only as good a remedy as the net worth of the Seller. In contrast, Title Insurance protects the insured Buyer from both the inconvenience of the legal dispute from any financial losses associated with the defective title. Title Insurance provides a solvent source of reimbursement if there is a warranty breach, and leaves the legal battle to the insurance company without risk to the new Buyer. THIS IS WHY TITLE INSURANCE IS PURCHASED BY MOST BUYERS.

B. Establishing "Merchantable Title" under State Law.

The professionals in the title business look to a "Base Title" or a "Root of Title" that is a compilation of the sequentially (chronologically) recorded documents found in the local government's public records that provide information on the ownership of the land for the last 30 or 40 years, or may go all the way back to the time that the State was admitted into the Union, and the lands were patented (sold) by the United States or prior sovereigns such as France (Florida and Louisiana) or Spain (also Louisiana and areas in the Western US).

These public records held by the local jurisdictions may be originals, or they may be copies which have been received from the parties, copied, indexed, and preserved for review. Cumulatively, these official records and documents are determinative of the ownership of land in the jurisdiction of each of the respective local governmental authorities.

In a practical sense, the recorded title documents, when searched and identified as relevant to the subject property, result in a "Title Abstract." In some states, the "Title Abstract" is a summary of the relevant recorded documents which is provided to a person qualified to provide title insurance on real property. In other states, these recorded documents are copied completely, compiled into a book-like volume (or volumes) and delivered from the Seller to the Buyer at the closing as proof of the Merchantable Title to the property. The new documents for the new closing are recorded and added to the formal Title Abstract for the new owner.

C. "Merchantable Title" and "Minerals", "Wind", and "Water."

In general, the determination of the "Merchantable Title" to a parcel of property will exclude the search and identification of claims on the property that relate to mineral ownership and exploitation, production, and removal of those minerals from the subject property. The rights to minerals and how the mineral owner "uses them or loses them" vary greatly among the states. In any case, the Buyer and the retained Broker and ultimately the title attorney or title company need to come together (before the purchase agreement is signed) and discuss the "Mineral Laws" of the state, and how the ownership of minerals in that state can affect the surface owner, as against the rights of a mineral owner.

It is not as critical to decide whether the purchase includes (or excludes) mineral rights on the property, so long as the Buyer knows whether minerals are included, in setting the final price and before signing the Buy/Sell Agreement. The Buyer needs to determine whether the property comes with the risks associated with mineral ownership by another party. Appropriate provisions dealing with mineral rights must be included in the Buy/Sell Agreement to allow the Buyer to protect the rights of use of the surface of the property.

Because of the possible ownership of "Mineral" rights by persons other than yourself, the rights that these third-party mineral owners may have over your prospective purchase must be identified, based upon the particular location of your property in the United States. For example, the following interests in the prospective property can be owned by third parties:

1. Oil and natural gas (i.e., liquid and gaseous hydrocarbons).

2. Coal, lignite (i.e., solid and semi-solid hydro-carbons).

3. Sand, gravel, timber (i.e., soil components).

4. Sulfur, gold, silver, bauxite, etc. (i.e., non-carbon minerals).

5. Wind rights (i.e., federally regulated and new issues).

6. Underground water rights and surface water rights.

Each of these property components or related uses are separately addressed under the laws of each state, detailing the relationship between the owner of these components and the surface owner. Therefore, a prospective Buyer's checklist of issues to investigate before finalizing negotiations of the terms of purchase (i.e., signing a Buy/Sell Agreement), is to identify if there are "Mineral" issues associated with the subject property, and to determine if and how those rights will affect the Buyer's intended uses of the property.

D. "Merchantable Title" And Risks That Are Not in the Public Records.

While establishing "Merchantable Title" is based upon the Public Record, there are several title risks that arise out of the Public Record which will still burden the subject property. In these cases, the purchase of Title Insurance provides the Buyer with protection from these claims. This type of servitudes or claims on the Property includes the following:

1. Unconstitutional tax sales.

Mennonite Board of Missions v. Adams, 462 U.S. 791, 103 S. Ct. 2706 (1983). These "Due Process" claims have been the procedural death to the local and municipal tax sale process. This has resulted in many Title Companies being unwilling to issue Title Insurance on property that includes a "Tax Deed" that was not done with actual notice to the taxpayer. If the subject property is a Mennonite Property, there will be real issues raised in resolving this defect.

2. Undisclosed heirs in previous probates (e.g., undisclosed adopted sibling).

3. Forgeries - directly or forged power of attorney.

4. State inheritance taxes liens.

5. Labor and material liens on property upon which the improvement was made, but the laborer or supplier has not been paid.

In each of these cases, the usual Public Record does not provide notice of the claim, but the Title Insurance does provide the Buyer with financial protection from the adverse effect such a claim would otherwise have. While these risks as adverse events do not arise often, they do happen, and the Title Insurance provides protection from this potential financial burden being thrust on the unsuspecting and unrelated party.

Different Procedures in Different States to Determine "Merchantable Title."

A. Public Records and Determination of "Merchantable Title."

It is interesting to note that between the fifty states of the Union, the determination of "Merchantable Title" for land within a given state has not developed into a uniform procedure. However, the procedure adopted by the various states can be classified generally into three types of procedural requirements to prove "Merchantable Title":

1. Strict public record determination.

2. Public record notice plus actual notice (third-party, in good faith).

3. Notorious possession, the passage of time, the cumulative legal effect.

In some states, the determination of "Merchantable Title" is based strictly on what is present on the public record. This is true even if a party (a new Buyer) knows that the Seller has already signed a deed selling the property to another person, but it has not been recorded. In the States that rely strictly on the public records review (without regard to knowledge), the determination of who has "Merchantable Title" is largely unaffected by any "He said, she said" disputes, or any off-the-record claims of intent different than the declarations of the recorded documents, that arise after a purchase concerning title to a particular parcel of property of the Seller. This public policy position is taken to allow any Buyer to rely on the public record without being threatened by unrecorded claims that can follow the real estate to the new Buyer.

These states usually deal with any fraud or "tomfoolery" between persons which occurs off the record, by allowing a personal claim for damages by the unrecorded claimant against the recorded Owner/Seller who has taken advantage of the unsophisticated buyer who did not know to record his acquisition of the parcel of property. But these claims between the disputing parties do not attach to the real property, which is transferred unconditionally according to the terms of the public record.

Alternatively, in some states, in the legal action filed to determine "Merchantable Title" of the real property, the Courts will allow the consideration of a party's knowledge of the facts "on the ground" or "off the public record" to determine if the party relied on matters beyond the public record. On the one hand, this public policy allows the exposure of persons conducting transactions in ways that take advantage of unsophisticated owners, or persons who do not know to record their documents to protect their claims. For example, if a Buyer knows that the property is occupied by a person who believes they are buying the property from the owner "on a handshake" or by an agreement that has never been recorded, the strict recordation state will deny protection of the unrecorded claims, while the other states may not allow the Buyer with knowledge of the prior interest to take advantage of the unrecorded claimant.

B. "Merchantable Title" and Stale Claims and Rights.

Many state laws of real estate recognize, in a general law sense, the doctrine of "Laches", which provides that rights that a person might otherwise hold or have will be lost (no longer recognized by law) if the holder of those rights delays in asserting those against others who clearly are exercising their own rights over the land. Other states, including Louisiana, address this concept through the principles of "Prescription" of the right if not asserted. To avoid the loss of property rights, clear uses of land that amount to a public declaration of ownership can preserve one's right to the property. These acts include exclusive physical use such as controlling hunting, conducting cultivation, grazing of livestock, cutting timber, exclusive control of possession such as through leases or timber leases, personal occupancy, and the collection of rents or other income.

Regardless of the strictness or openness of the state's procedure, the state will still have mechanisms by which any un-asserted rights will ultimately be lost. Many of these states have adopted their version of the uniform "Marketable Title of Record Act" to eliminate un-asserted claims with the running of time. There are sound public policy and economic policy reasons for preserving actual claims of third parties in land for a reasonable time. However, there are equally sound public policy and economic policy reasons to establish clear rules where (1) real rights, are un-asserted for long periods, and (2) where rights arise inadvertently by technical errors in the conveyance documents. These clouds and claims on the property should expire and terminate if not asserted.

These laws are very practical, and affirmatively support the protection and re-establishment of "Merchantable Title" to land with the passage of law. In other words, the law requires that owners "Use It or Lose It."

C. Prospective Buyer's Due Diligence on Title Issues.

The best way to avoid such a title problem, or possession dispute, is to make sure that you, as the Buyer, or your Real Estate Broker, makes a physical inspection of the subject property, to identify any possessors, lessees, or other persons present on the subject property. Equally, the physical inspection will make sure that any unexpected uses, activities, or improvements are identified. This information will provide a Buyer with the opportunity to avoid a title dispute or a use dispute which could have been avoided by a good inspection.

Who Pays for "Owner's Title Insurance" in Your State?

One of the many "first" questions that a Buyer should ask the Real Estate Broker is "Who pays for Title Insurance in this State: the Buyer or the Seller?" Obviously, the Title Insurance premium is a significant cost. The answer to this question can have a significant increased effect on the gross cost for a purchaser, or have a significant decrease in sale proceeds for the Seller. There is no right answer or wrong answer, but a Buyer needs to know early on in the negotiations what the local "expectations" will be on who normally pays this expense. Again, the Buyer's retained Real Estate Broker will know how to best use this issue to the Buyer's advantage.

Also, a Buyer who is interested in making sure that any title cloud or possible defect is identified and cured by the Seller should agree early to pay for the Title Insurance if this also allows the Buyer to choose the title attorney or title company. With this arrangement, the Buyer is assured to be fully informed of any quasi-cloud on the title. Conversely, as the Seller, controlling the production of the Title Insurance gives the Seller maximum control over the title search and the identification of any quasi-clouds that the Title Company might not require to be cured. In short, as long as the Buyer agrees to shoulder this expense, the Buyer can adjust the final offered purchase price to take that expense into consideration of the overall cost of the property. It is a net-net world in land pricing.

Conclusion: Does the New Owner Need "Owner's Title Insurance?"

Ultimately, like the purchase of any other "insurance" product, a Buyer must decide what financial risk he can afford to take, and whether or not the Buyer is better off with insurance to cover this asset risk. This insurance is not an insignificant cost, but it does provide financial protection for a classically insurable risk: a risk that has a low likelihood to occur, but causes very large financial damage when it does occur.

While I have not always agreed, my experience shows that the following three circumstances sometimes encourage a Buyer to save the premium and go "bareback" without Title Insurance:

1. The parcel's purchase price is small enough that the Buyer can financially afford to lose the money or has sufficient funds to clear up the title later. This arises when small parcels are being purchased, possibly for their immediate income.
2. If the Buyer has reliable personal knowledge of the Seller's family, the family members, and the probate orders identifying family members. This exception applies only if there is an uncomplicated family structure, the Seller is in good health and active, there are few or no step-parents, few or no step-children, and no transactions by the owners in the last ten years.
3. A very large mortgage has been placed on the property in the last five years that was not in a "loan workout" posture. Also, I would look to make sure that no recorded transactions have occurred since that large mortgage. Provided the Lender/Mortgagee is a traditional lender (such as owner financing or related business financing), then a Buyer may have a justification in not purchasing Title Insurance.

With few exceptions, it is my belief that the decision of whether or not to purchase Owner's Title Insurance is an "asset preservation" issue or a "financial" issue concerning the long-term protection of a Buyer's net worth. Who really wants to avoid the title insurance policy, and win the "negative" lottery with a bad title on a large piece of property? No one!

With any substantial acquisition, the financial peace of mind that arises from Owner's Title Insurance should be part of the enjoyment and security that comes with these large assets.

In short, it's my professional suggestion to let peace be with you, and buy that Owner's Title Insurance!

About Paul Hurd

Paul Loy Hurd is a licensed attorney and title agent with over thirty-five years of legal and title closing experience. He graduated in 1972 with a BA from Tulane University in New Orleans, Louisiana and graduated again from Tulane University School of Law with a J.D. in 1978. Mr. Hurd served for ten years as a Certified Bank Compliance Officer and General Counsel for a mid-sized regional bank before establishing his own private practice of law – Paul Loy Hurd, APLC – in Monroe, Louisiana. His practice focuses on consumer regulatory compliance, business formation and consulting, and real estate litigation. He has established a significant real estate transaction business and title agency through his company Home Title Guaranty. Mr. Hurd has three sons and is married to the greatest wife, Cathy Hurd.

Chapter 9 - Technology and the Land Search Process - By Ryan Folk

The Old School Way of Searching for Land

It's difficult to envision, especially for first-time land buyers or those yet to embark on their quest to find the perfect piece of land, but 15+ years ago searching for land was an entirely different process. It entailed much more time and effort. If asked to describe what searching for land was like back then, I'd sum it up in just a few words. Cumbersome. Tedious. Frustrating. It required a lot of legwork. I think it's fair to say that no one wants to go back to the "good old days", given that would-be land buyers had very few tools at their disposal. Technology has evolved so much in the last two decades. Buyers should be grateful for how much easier searching for property has become.

Twenty years ago, would-be buyers couldn't dial-up an experienced land agent affiliated with a high-profile land brokerage firm like buyers have the option of doing today. They could call on a real estate agent who knew the local market, but there were very few real estate agents that specialized in land sales. Agents who sold residential homes lacked the knowledge and experience needed to assist buyers in a land transaction.

In the pre-internet era, buyers who were searching for land to purchase had to buy a newspaper and search through the classifieds. Just imagine the time spent driving around in a truck with a physical road map spread across the dash, scouting for listing signs, For Sale by Owner (FSBO) signs, or trudging down to the courthouse to retrieve property records. The process was exasperating, to say the least.

Real estate agents and sellers used to control access to property information. Not only did they hold all the cards, but they also played close to the chest. Back then the land search process was a different ballgame, but the buyer versus seller playing field has gradually been tilting towards advantage buyer.

The Internet and Land Listing Sites Pave the Way

Ahh, the joy of sitting down at your clunky desktop PC to search the internet in the mid-90s. At that time the dial-up noises were a glorious symphony and having a family member kick you off the internet to use the phone just came with the territory. The emergence of the internet in the mid-90s created an explosion of online information that was available at the click of a mouse to anyone who was interested in purchasing real estate. It completely changed the way real estate land transactions occur.

It used to be that the Multiple Listing Service (MLS), which is a database of listing information, was only accessible by licensed real estate agents. But around 1994, the MLS went public, and real estate agents were no longer the gatekeepers of listing information.

Consumers became hungry for information, and they needed more information to make a buying decision – more information than the MLS could provide. Buyers wanted information such as homes and land that were for sale by owner and value estimates, which local agents typically prepared for their clients in the form of a Comparative Market Analysis (CMA).

By the early 2000s, consumers were braving the internet at record speed – like cowboys galloping towards a brave new world. The internet had revolutionized the way would-be buyers searched for land. With consumers steering the demand, new specialty, third-party websites like ForSaleByOwner.com, Zillow, Trulia, and Redfin sprang up overnight, leveraging consumers' insatiable appetite for information.

The new websites were a valuable online resource for buyers and provided local market information, home estimates, and online communities. However, the MLS, Zillow, Trulia, and Redfin focused on marketing existing homes, not raw land. They catered to the residential home buyer, not those looking for rural property. There was a need for an online listing website that showcased *only* land that was for sale across the United States. Though LandandFarm.com was the first rural property website to launch in 1998, it wasn't until the mid-2000s that the need for a land listing site was truly realized.

Modern Tools and Resources for Every Land Buyer

There is certainly no shortage of options to help buyers locate land these days. Today's buyers are doing their own research online long before they pick up the phone and call an agent. Modern technology, including websites, blogs, apps, mapping, and even social media have made the land search process virtually seamless, as retrieving information has become more "push" than "pull." There is a plethora of information living in mobile apps. Our location, habits, and personal taste and preferences are used to "push" relevant content and suggestions our way. The utilization of mobile devices gives people easy access to information anywhere and everywhere. Before hitting the backroads looking for land with an agent, buyers are able to narrow down their desires and options, and eliminate properties that don't fit their requirements.

There are many digital tools and resources to help bolster your land search, and choosing which websites and tools are worth your time can be a challenge in itself. I've done that for you here, and it will hopefully turn your land-buying experience into a walk in the park. Listed below are a few good places to start:

Land Listing Websites

Quite a few land-for sale-platforms have popped up to meet the needs of land buyers and sellers- LANDFLIP.com, LandWatch.com, LandsofAmerica.com, and LandandFarm.com are among the best. Buyers will find most of the same listings and information on each of these sites, but the way it's presented is drastically different. As the Founder and CEO of LANDFLIP, I can say we strive to stay ahead of the pack, implementing cutting-edge technology and creating new features people have come to expect.

LANDFLIP boasts strong visual appeal, a top-notch search mechanism, and a massive selection of land for sale by both real estate agents and private sellers. Buyers can easily peruse land for sale, land auctions, and land for lease. Users can create a free buyer profile, giving them the ability to save listings, manage land preferences, and receive alerts from land sellers when listings match their set preferences. LANDFLIP has proven to be a comprehensive resource for land buyers and investors searching for hunting land, farmland, home sites, timberland, horse farms, waterfront, ranches, and other types of land.

Most land-only websites employ advanced search features, enabling buyers to hone-in on very specific types of acreage. All the top-tier land listing sites allow sellers to upload drone footage, which gives an amazing aerial view of the entire property as well as the surrounding areas. Buyers can check out parcel maps, terrain maps, topography maps, satellite images, and see defined property boundary lines. Sophisticated mapping tools allow you to overlay property boundaries onto different map types. Most land listing sites will also have a directory of brokers across the country who specialize in selling rural land.

Websites and Blogs for All Things Land

Buying land for the first time can be a bit daunting; knowledge and first-hand experiences from the right people offer buyers added reassurance. Luckily, there are authoritative sources out there that are jam-packed with insight, news, and advice – and not only for first-time buyers. Most of the top blogs cover hot-button news, market trends, and land ownership topics, in addition to anything and everything having to do with the buying and selling process.

After the real estate market crash, I realized people were still interested in purchasing land, but one thing had changed. Buyers and investors were smarter than ever before. They needed a portal that offered a wide variety of information and covered all areas of the land industry. In 2008, I developed LandThink (LANDFLIP's sister site). LandThink visitors can browse a variety of land categories such as Buying, Selling, Owning, and Living. In 2012, the "Pulse" was launched to gather interesting insight into the current land real estate market. It was designed to be fun and interesting for subscribers, fans, and followers, while providing a "pulse" of the ever-changing land market. With a panel of contributors that boasts some of the most respected professionals in their field, LandThink continues to gain popularity among industry professionals and land enthusiasts.

The REALTORS® Land Institute Blog features pertinent land information and advice from their own Accredited Land Consultants (ALCs). This is a prestigious designation that requires successful completion of a rigorous education program and a proven track record of transaction performance. One of the newest blogs available for buyers, Rethink:Rural, "celebrates the virtues of country living and helps those who are searching for a rural lifestyle find the answers they need." Many of the most recognized land brokerage firms, such as Mossy Oak Properties, National Land Realty, and Southeastern Land Group have blogs showcasing articles and videos designed to assist potential customers in their purchasing decision.

Google Earth

Google Earth is a free mapping program that combines satellite images, maps, and aerial shots, and it is a great land scouting tool. Users can zoom-in to any physical address and investigate the topography of the land. It also provides a 3D rendering of the satellite data and StreetView. Buyers can also overlay Google Maps in Google Earth, as well as share and save searches.

Sex Offender Registries

Whether you're buying land in a neighborhood or a rural parcel on which to build your dream home, it's important to know if there are sex offenders living in the vicinity. There are two major sex offender registries available online.

The United States Department of Justice National Sex Offender Public Website is a national registry that recently launched a mobile app, so it's easier than ever to search the archives by name or location. You can view the current addresses and photos of all registered sex offenders. A second option is Family Watchdog. This is a free, nongovernment site to help locate registered sex offenders. It gathers data from various state registries, plus you can sign up to receive a notification when offenders move into or out of the area.

Social Media

Everyone is on social media, and it has emerged as a great way to share information, advice, photos, and ideas about your land buying journey. More and more buyers are reaching out to their family, co-workers, and friends for buying tips and recommendations on brokerage firms, agents, lenders, and more. Following the business pages of local brokerage firms and agents on social platforms like Facebook and Twitter provides insight into how connected they are to the local land market.

Public Property Records Database

Real estate transactions are public record and can be searched on the county tax assessor's website. In most places, the tax assessor's office and the county clerk maintain the database. You can search the website free of charge, but the recorder's database usually requires a visit in person. You will need a property address or the owner's name to search the database. A quick search can reveal detailed information like value, sales history, ownership, square footage (if there's a structure), improvements, and more. Liens, short sale pay off amounts, and any other debts against the property can be revealed in a search using the owner's name or property address. To verify that improvements and additions to the property were done legally, it may be necessary to contact the city/county planning and zoning department.

School and District Ranking Websites

Whether or not you have school-age children, buying land within a highly desirable school district can help preserve value and speed up the rate of resale. Opinions on school districts and rankings is the one area in which a REALTOR® isn't much help to a buyer. They will usually provide basic information like the school district in which a particular property is located. Because honest opinions could be construed as "steering" under the Fair Housing Act, it's good practice for REALTORS® to refer buyers to third-party sources and let them make their own choices. The National Center of Educational Statistics (NCES) is the primary federal entity for collecting and analyzing data related to education. GreatSchools.org is a national nonprofit that provides school ratings, test scores, and reviews regarding the caliber of the teaching.

Benefits of Hiring an Experienced Land Agent

Back when I was actively selling land, I'd always chuckle a little bit inside when buyers would show up to look at land with "their agent," and he would be driving a shiny sports car, wearing slacks and expensive loafers, or she showed up in a dress and high heels expecting to walk the property. While this attire is appropriate for the closing table, it's not for a rural property showing. Real estate has many fields, and each one requires special knowledge and expertise. There is even specialization of agents within the land industry, such as commercial, farmland, and ranch property specialists.

Don't get me wrong, I would never downplay the importance of residential agents, but buyers and sellers of rural land who don't seek the guidance of an experienced land agent are doing themselves a huge disservice. Land transactions are more difficult and complex than residential transactions. Land brokerage is an area of real estate that requires an agent who possess a special skill set. You can count on every land transaction to have a wrinkle – some big enough to kill the deal if not handled properly. As a buyer, you need an agent who is committed to protecting your interests, clearly understands your objectives, and adheres to a strict code of ethics.

A buyer should always take advantage of hiring an experienced land agent when possible. The agreement can be terminated at any time, and the buyer is not responsible for the agent's commission. The seller has an agreement with the listing broker, and the commission is paid from the proceeds of the sale. In rare circumstances, if the property being purchased is For Sale by Owner (FSBO) and the seller refuses to pay the buyer's agent a commission, then the buyer may have to pay the agent out of their own pocket. Remember commission is *always* negotiable, and whether or not a buyer pays for an agent's services should be spelled out in a Buyer Brokerage Agreement.

When considering a property, a buyer doesn't always know the right questions to ask. It is a land agent's job to utilize every tool in their arsenal to discover every aspect of a property being presented to a buyer. There is a different evaluation process for land than for residential real estate. Land comes with a different set of considerations such as:

- Percolation tests
- Zoning
- Boundaries
- Elevation
- Surveys to determine property access
- Conservation easements
- Wetland restrictions
- Wildlife habitat
- Mineral rights
- Covenants and Restrictions
- Soil types
- Farm and crop productivity
- Timber values
- Site preparation
- Access to utilities
- Neighborhood, amenities, and school districts (which affect resale value)

Don't hesitate to do some research before enlisting the services of a land agent. In addition to experience, look for agents that carry special designations or are members of the REALTORS® Land Institute. A strong knowledge of timberland, forestry, geology, or soil science could be helpful, depending on the type of transaction.

A good land agent will help a buyer determine the "highest and best use", and can also help secure financing on a land loan. Land agents have a very close network of professionals that they work with on a regular basis – attorneys, lenders, foresters, surveyors, tax professionals, custom builders, land-clearing companies, and wetland and environmental consultants. Armed with their extensive knowledge of the area and current market conditions, they will help clients narrow down the list of potential properties, negotiate the best price, and handle the large amount of paperwork involved from contract through closing.

There is no substitute for the professional services a reputable land brokerage firm can offer a land buyer. An agent who deals with land all the time can help you avoid pitfalls during or after closing and help ensure a smooth, successful transaction.

If You Want It, Buy It

I think it's impossible for some to stop overthinking. Personally, I've never been the type of guy to flip a coin for every big decision in my life; making a big decision has never pained me. Unfortunately, when it comes to pulling the trigger on a piece of land, some people spend entirely too much time endlessly obsessing over the decision. While the decision to buy a property is one that should never be taken lightly, the analyzing and second-guessing can paralyze a would-be land buyer into a state of total inaction. This inability to make any forward progress has a name; it's a syndrome known as analysis paralysis. Often the agent will candidly ask the customer to buy the property, and open up a serious line of conservation with the buyer regarding their desire to own the property.

Most land agents would agree that there is absolutely nothing wrong with asking a customer to buy a property. But – and that's a big but – it's up to land agents and brokers to arm their customers and clients with enough information to get them to the point where they realize why it makes sense for them to purchase the property. As land agents, it's our duty to help would-be buyers see the value in the purchase and help them reach a certain level of comfort with their decision to buy.

Earlier this summer, I stumbled on an article published on LinkedIn, written by one of their senior news editors. The article was about an ad epiphany noted actor Will Smith recently had. Smith made the statement "If people don't want it, you're not going to be able to sell it." He is absolutely correct. A good land agent, whom you want to assist you in a transaction, will help you see the value in a potential purchase and help you as a buyer come to a conclusion. That is, *do you want the property?*

After the due diligence and systematic research has been completed, it comes down to a simple question. As Jonathan Goode, a land agent with Southeastern Land Group pointed out in his article published on LandThink titled *Do You Want It?*, "When you have looked at a property and asked all of the right questions, there comes a point when you have to make a decision: *Do you want it?*" Failing to make a timely decision can cost you the piece of land you want and cause you to miss out on a good opportunity.

So when is the right time for a buyer to ask themselves if they want a piece of property?

In his article, Jonathan Goode poses four questions that buyers should answer first.

1. **Is this the right location?**
2. **Does it fit your needs?**
3. **How are you going to pay for it?**
4. **Do you want it?**

Purchasing land as an investment or to build your dream home is a smart financial strategy. If bought at the right price, land is an inexpensive investment and a smart place to park your cash. It sits there quietly and usually requires little to no maintenance. Investing in land can provide enjoyment and peace of mind, if buyers understand that land is not liquid and are prepared to hold on to the property for the long term.

If the answer to the above questions is a resounding "yes", then make a bold move towards the end zone. Make the land yours. As a buyer, don't let the fear of what MIGHT happen keep you from purchasing land that would enrich your life and bring joy to you and your family. If the answer to number four is "no", then you need to keep looking.

There will always be unanswered questions. But remember, a land purchase is not an irreversible or life-altering decision. If you want it, buy the dirt and don't look back after that. Life is full of surprises. Enjoy them.

About Ryan Folk

After graduating from Jacksonville State University with a BS in Computer Information Systems, Ryan Folk began his career in the dot-com industry. He spent 6 years traveling the country, selling and implementing supply chain and HR software solutions for various Fortune 1000 companies. Luckily, just as the big tech bubble started to burst, a former colleague introduced Ryan to a new career – selling land. Within a month, he was a licensed real estate agent, and on day one had his first land listing. Ryan's only dilemma...where to advertise?

In March of 2004, Ryan put his tech know-how back to work and developed LANDFLIP to market his personal listings. The site brought buyers, and soon he had sold over $30 million in land transactions. Increasingly, other agents expressed an interest in advertising on LANDFLIP. In the summer of 2007, the decision was made to convert LANDFLIP into a paid listing site. It continues to grow as one of today's top land-for-sale marketing platforms.

Wrapping it All Up

Thank you for reading my humble little book.

I hope you got an idea or two that will help you with your next land purchase. Feel free to contact any of these guys with questions. They have provided information about themselves in the last paragraph of each chapter to help you find them.

Please take a minute to provide a review of my book. I believe you got plenty of value for the cost in this deal, so I'd be grateful for your help in giving this book a little notice so it can be useful to others, too. If you provide a review, then send me an email letting me know – we'll ship you a nice little gift to say thanks.

At RecLand Realty, all we do is land. Let us know when we can serve you. We can be found pretty easily by going to www.RecLand.net. Our video blog is at www.RecLandTalks.com. You can also find out what we're up to at www.facebook.com/recland and www.twitter.com/reclandrealty. I am always accessible by email at patlporter@bellsouth.net.

Remember, this information is provided as-is and does not in any way make or imply any guarantees as to an outcome. You will need to evaluate the information herein and consult the appropriate professionals such as surveyors, attorneys, tax accountants, or any other professional or agency to acquire the information and guidance you need to help you make the decision that is best for you.

Pat Porter, Broker

RecLand Realty, LLC – 410 Olive Street – Monroe, LA 71201

Other real estate and land books by Pat Porter:

"How to Sell Your Land Faster – Proven Ways to Improve the Value & Desirability of Rural Land" is available in ebook, paperback, and audio at Amazon at https://www.amazon.com/How-Sell-Your-Land-Faster/dp/1534614915

"The Stuff the Best Land Agents Do: And You Should Do Them, Too!" is available in ebook and audio at Amazon at https://www.amazon.com/Stuff-Best-Land-Agents-Do-ebook/dp/B01JVET6NM

"Land Mines: Lessons to Keep Your Rural Real Estate Deals From Blowing Up" is available in ebook & audio at Amazon at https://www.amazon.com/Land-Mines-Lessons-Estate-Blowing-ebook/dp/B01NAQMFHF

Or just visit my author page at http://amazon.com/author/recland-pat-porter

Made in the USA
Las Vegas, NV
31 August 2022